Skeleton Keys

Other books by the author

Poetry
Robe Of Skin
Milesian Fables
Out Of Exile
Cat Kin
Safe Levels
Living Jazz
Beautiful Is Enough
Omnibus Occasions
Selected Poems 1956-96

Novels
The Summer Ghosts
Zones
A Sleeping Partner
Strange Alphabet
The Stump
Instrument Of Pleasure
The Drive North
Last Throes
Scrubbers

Non-fiction
Jean Rhys Revisited

Translations
Maldoror & Complete Works (Lautréamont)
Days And Nights (Jarry)
Flesh Unlimited: Three Novels (Apollinaire & Aragon)
Masochism In America (Mac Orlan)
Surrealist Games (Breton, Eluard, etc)
Heliogabalus (Artaud)

SKELETON KEYS

ALEXIS LYKIARD

2003

Skeleton Keys is published by
Redbeck Press, 24 Aireville Road,
Frizinghall, Bradford BD9 4HH.

Typeset by Kath Leaver,
67 Moorhead Crescent, Moorhead,
Shipley, West Yorkshire BD18 4LQ.
Tel: 07976 950 447
email: kath.leaver@btinternet.com

Design and print by Tony Ward,
Arc & Throstle Press, Nanholme Mill,
Shaw Wood Road, Todmorden,
Lancashire OL14 6DA

All rights reserved. No part of this book
may be reproduced in any form except
by a newspaper or magazine reviewer who
wishes to quote brief passages in
connection with a review.

Copyright © Alexis Lykiard 2003

Skeleton Keys
ISBN 1-904338-04-6

A CIP catalogue record for this book is
available from the British Library.

ACKNOWLEDGEMENTS
Some of these poems first appeared in the
following magazines: *Acumen; Ambit;
Dirty Goat (USA); Exeter Flying Post;
The Frogmore Papers; Granta; Haiku
Quarterly; London Magazine; Penniless Press;
Poetry Salzburg Review; The Poet's Voice;
The Rialto; Tears In The Fence.*

Cover photo:
   Soldiers and civilians on the Acropolis, 1943
   (Bundesarchiv, Koblenz)

*In memory of my mother, Maria Casdagli (1910-1963)
and her brother, my uncle, Alexis Casdagli (1907-1997)*

"... Oh, I should doubt," she exclaimed, "whether there's any such thing as an innocent secret! Whatever has been buried, surely, corrupts? Nothing keeps innocence innocent but daylight. A truth's just a truth, to start with, with no particular nature, good or bad – but how can any truth not go bad from being underground? Dug up again after years and laid on the mat, it's inconvenient, shocking – apart from anything else there's no place left in life for it any more. To dig up somebody else's truth for them would seem to me sheer malignancy; to dig up one's own madness – I never would."

Elizabeth Bowen: **The Heat Of The Day**, 1949

Time to turn memory's key on the dirty cellar
And scorn the clichés of the lark ascending
Everything clean and dry as interstellar
Space. This is the happy ending.

Randall Swingler: **The God In The Cave**, 1950

Contents

Introduction – 9
Living Art – 11
What My Father Did – 12
Disinherited – 13
Diaspora, Of Sorts – 14
Observation – 16
Mikis Theodorakis – 17
The Getting Of Wisdom – 18
Survival Of The Fascist – 19
Voices From The Past – 21
Perivoli – 22
At Chora Sphakion – 26
One Side Of 'The Family' – 26
Old Warrior – 27
First Hand Accounts – 28
Afternoon In Anopolis – 30
Goatsong – 32
By Souda Bay – 33
The Point At Loutro – 34
Omonia In The 1960s – 36
Academic Questions (i.m. C. A. Trypanis) – 38
A Diva – 40
The Formalities – 41
Albanian Jokes – 42
Kneecaps – 43
Singing Life (i.m. Sotiria Bellou) – 44
Civil Wars Are Worst – 47
Interrogation – 48
Last Respects – 52

INTRODUCTION

My previous writing often concerned itself with family roots, diverse socio-cultural backgrounds, apprenticeship and travel, beloved friends and despised enemies – including a variety of unexpected encounters. But these largely autobiographical books were mostly in prose. *Skeleton Keys* addresses the implicit confusions of autobiography in poetic terms. I've tried to change tack and journey further, to make a voyage back through private and public history. The more time passed of course, the more imperative it seemed to reconsider or possibly rediscover my own Greek origins.

War, civil strife, military dictatorship and other disasters are inevitably reflected, touched on directly or obliquely. So it may be helpful here to mention a few historical markers, some of which are referred to in various poems.

The Greek War of Independence (1821-1827) finally freed most of Greece from centuries of Turkish occupation. For the Great Powers, then as now, impoverished little Greece had a disproportionately large strategic and symbolic value. It was seen as necessary to European stability that 19th and 20th century Greek history should be monarchical: a hybrid bunch of Euro-royals was duly imported. After Independence, the first King of Greece installed was Otho of Bavaria (1833-1862). Ironically enough for Greece, every kind of upheaval followed during the years prior to World War I – the Balkan wars, assassinations, revolutions, coups and abdications, military dictatorships... In 1922 came the Asia Minor débâcle, the sack of Smyrna, the Turkish slaughter of countless Greeks and Armenians, and the subsequent diaspora of survivors to the Greek mainland and elsewhere.

The year 1940 – the tail-end of the Metaxas dictatorship, during which I was born – marked that extraordinary period of World War II when Greece was Britain's only ally, staunchly routing the Italian invasion before being overwhelmed by German military might. But at the end of the German Occupation in autumn 1944, a devastating Civil War was precipitated which continued until autumn 1949. Churchill and Stalin in differently ruthless ways had sold out their gallant and over-idealistic supporters the Greeks. The opportunity of becoming a republic was denied. There were to be no properly democratic elections: the Left felt betrayed, witnessing internment for its partisans and rewards for racketeers and collaborators.

The savagery was prolonged and extreme. Even a full generation later the abiding legacy of the Civil War was still more poisonous fruit. Once again, democratic elections (with a landslide victory envisaged for the Left) were forestalled, to be replaced by a fascist military coup. The ensuing Greek Colonels' dictatorship from 1967-1974 was shamefully allowed to drag on by certain major powers, for after all weren't the Colonels always conveniently reminding Greeks of their own worthy anti-Communist and Christian credentials? One of the few positive results of seven years of national repression and injustice was the departure – albeit by default – of the fatuous playboy King Constantine. Greece neither wanted nor needed any more royal families, wherever they originated from. In any case, small poor countries cannot afford top-heavy, repressive or corrupt rule, in whatever form it presents itself.

Getting rid of both military and monarchical rule meant Greeks regained their pride: the nation could look to the future with more confidence. But pride in being Greek has its price: this wonderful, wounded land somehow scars her children for life. The wanderer invariably returns, though. Hence these reassessments of family ties serve to underline how truth and lies are relative at last: one must try to thread through the labyrinth like some latter-day Theseus, slowly finding a way out of the darkness. And onward – past the elusive dreams and false memories, all those tortuous politics and outworn myths – until the confrontation with what, in the end, was always instinctively guessed from the beginning.

Of course there's no sure exorcism, artful or artless. Yet explorations if not explanations (alongside apologies and celebrations, perhaps) are in order from time to time; they help one make sense of the seeming contingency or meaninglessness of life. Every family possesses its dark secrets and locked doors, lies, betrayals, closeted skeletons and unquiet ghosts. Hatred and heroism, greed, deceit and honour: Greeks throughout history have offered archetypal examples of extreme behaviour within the family. Mine is no exception, on either side. Now some things unspoken do need speaking of; some secrets no longer need keeping, if they ever did. *Skeleton Keys* tries to relate the kindness or unkindness of both close and distant kin. It marks a return to the troubled landscapes of my birth. Whether these people, places and events are any the clearer or truer for being translated into poetic form, is for readers to judge.

Living Art

    We all descend toward the dark,
falling precipitate as each day goes.
During this dream-life, daring death,
where none can afford to hoard a breath
        men seem to count for less than dominoes.

    Heart-sick and prey to dread, a dreamer knows
artistry's hard-won yet it will endure
by keeping sight of what continues –
constant determination to resist
        the state of evil or the evil State.

    The strife demands a bitter toll, its mark
is to demand exemplars, fittest to create
from love. These volunteers, at first not missed,
must soon engage an enemy undeterred,
        despite and in full knowledge of, long odds.

    Stern thankless task, embodying the pure…
Champions of mere mortality placate no gods,
believe in being aware. Confronting Fate
they – soldier, civilian, prisoner or free –
        won't crack, won't betray. (A war-child like me

    learned their hard languages, whose allied words
helped shape a better world.) They're living thought,
the loving truth-tellers, themselves cut short.
Remember Europeans your poet-heroes:
    Farewell to Douglas, *Adieu* Desnos!

[i.m. Keith Douglas 1920-1944. Normandy.
 i.m. Robert Desnos 1900-1945. Terezin.]

What My Father Did

One jingle ran: *What does your father do?*
Conundrum some affluent ruffians would
come out with too often and pose, grinning.
At an unanswerable boarding school,
faced with their hateful, uninventive jeers
or idle rich curiosity, I'd play the fool.
(Hard luck, your elders had it in for you.)
It seemed untrue, did less convincing good
to mutter then what I'd been told to say,
that my father had recently *retired*...
A mumbled word. Inadequate beginning.
Trigger for bad rhymes, jibes employed: "Oh, *fired*,
he means – young Lick Yard, Like Yid, whatsisname!"

Retired? A tricky verb, not plain enough.
Just you come clean, play straight and take the blame,
lay off the greasy-Greek pathetic guff!
"Hang on," somebody'd crow, "retired from *where*?"
Or *whence*, I'd think. (Amid grim teenage fears
was dread of being corrected, while to me
cricketers were True Brits at any rate...)
Inquisitors always grow bored: they too
tired of such dull sport and gave up on me.
Brainwashed, I never learned why he'd 'retired',
mid-forties, to safe haven over here.
Survival was one's only aim: what's done
can't be owned up to... Peacetime kept a son

observing curfew at a country school,
ungainly runt resigned to alien fate.
(Dubbin on Corps boots, endless good clean fun.)
Officers-and-Gents define retirement
as voluntary finish of fine innings,
not gutless early exit from the fray.
As for my toffee-nosed tormentors, they
most likely thought 'retired', that vague term, meant
opting out – honoured by The Family Firm,
opinions ossified, old boys at ill-earned rest,
boozily counting misbegotten gains.
High Tory public school types cannot guess
more private facts of life, the secret lives

all exiles must make shift to justify
when nowhere's left to go, to hide or run.
Stoic and stooge, I did my time, trapped by
a past I knew too little of. Yet childhood days
stay foreign to me still, escape again...
(There's no reply. What *did* my father do?)
For certain things that slippery conman did,
as wartime collaborator and crook,
he tried to make me and my mother pay.
Poetic justice clears our sad prosaic debts:
the shame she lived with, which we couldn't share;
her generosity cut short. Life isn't fair.
Others were hurt too, by his overbearing

hate. Now definitively he's retired,
his last departure marked here by this book.

DISINHERITED

>   *... et mon luth constellé*
>   *Porte le* soleil *noir de la* Mélancolie.

Nerval was an early literary hero, years ago.
One of my first published pieces, heartfelt adolescent verse,
had his despair and suicide for lonely theme.

Never, though, in my tenebrously teenage dream
did I guess legacies might move from bad to even worse,
so I'd be left only that echoed epithet, in code,
>   El Desdichado.

Diaspora, of Sorts

My fascist father's only 'work',
his last word and his final work,
selfish employment of so many years,
would lie in handing out,

distributing to distant others
piecemeal, a strange largesse.
Possessions never truly his to give –
the missing parts of my own life…

Such false generosity meant I'd not be
allowed to know or to suspect, to have
or to recall. Quite calculatingly
he plied a sort of gainful trade:

ill deeds and bygones, all were
reduced, alike disposed of. He
proved a dab hand at the gradual
dispersal of old objects. Things

of value first, then sentimental trivia
filled with secrets, were to disappear.
Their absence spelt his guilt. He knew
the price fools set on odds and ends.

Trinkets my dead mother wore –
inscribed books – a fine silk scarf
she favoured – photo albums – all
flotsam of peculiar circumstance.

Family relics bit by bit became
relics contemptible, *triste*, unfamiliar…
Nothing was left me, other than
a clutch of adult toys gone rotten,

various partial artefacts acquired
only with difficulty, awkwardly.
Worthless items, pieced together, what
no one else 'in his right mind' could want.

These were the very scraps I treasured, then
through questioning persistence
or by chance, and via memory's
impoverished retrieval system, found.

Later, I tried notating alien words,
whose music, if diminished, remains audible...
Now curiously one sticks with broken
remnants of the physical, still

in the hope of finding how to honour
those priceless, unforgotten names
that counted once and always for so much.
What if the owners of poor scattered things

were able to return – each ancestor restored
to breath, with each in fairest form
admitting to the mind more generous
legacies? However burdensome, amends

of kindness might at last be made,
accounts of kinship settled, due attention paid
my long-lost mother, for just one. Among
so many others, the dead lovers, friends.

Observation

Wherever I travel, volunteered Seferis,
Greece keeps wounding me.
So there are no safe harbours,
as every Greek acknowledges.
And for all such compulsive voyagers
in time the Fates were invented, to pursue
each individual through a history
of mortal failings and catastrophe.

There was once a goggle-eyed conscript
who witnessed the sack of Smyrna,
watching it from the safety of his ship.
Did those screams dated 1922
occasionally invade his dreams?
Greeks and Armenians trying to flee,
men, women, children, of whom none
was destined to be spared.

Turks, in the picturesque old phrase,
put the entire town's population
to the sword. Distant, mythical days...
My father, always the fortunate survivor,
seems to have seen out national service
on a firmly detached, a passive note.
I heard him once observe in company
that nothing at all could have been done.

Everyone doubtless obeyed orders
or made excuses for what should never
have happened in the first place, nor, come
to that, in this or any other place:
civilians massacred because of some
mad chimera of Nationalism. Then
the hordes of refugees from Asia Minor
reached Greece, only to be displaced forever.

Mikis Theodorakis

> And therefore what afflicts you? Why to heare
> The Fate of Greece and Ilion mourne you so?
> The Gods have done it; as to all they do
> Destine destruction, that from thence may rise
> A Poeme to instruct posterities.
> *Homer's Odyssey,* tr. *George Chapman, 1614-15*

Inspiring, disconcerting too, to hear
him talk about those times
long gone, abysmal days

of '67. What vast distance
in the strangely slow, pained utterance
of half-familiar words,

lilt of a lost mother-tongue
I strained just to decipher
with the doubtful aid of French

subtitles... Flickering TV screen
at two a.m. inside a darkened
Dieppe hotel room.

He murmurs as you dream. I'm
entranced, watching him rehearse
The Sun And Time

alongside German rock musicians,
Greek bouzouki players,
some of them not even born

when first he got by heart
almost three dozen poems
for his song cycle of the soul.

Epic composed in solitary.
The cell a sounding-board,
his craft trying not to founder

amid screams or dreadful silence.
He played out the whole work
piece by piece within himself.

Not to disintegrate, go mad
nor to go under. Somehow
he set harmonious sail. A man

who'd sung of Occupation,
fratricidal war, the prison islands,
torture and TB. Hunger, thirst,

all forms of suffering he knew.
Those nameless cowards coveting
his fame could never break him:

such creatures as despise creation,
envy everyone who moves
lovingly, serenely toward myth

without – and far beyond – them.

The Getting of Wisdom

Epimenides, wrote one ancient commentator,
wandered into a nymph-haunted cave on Crete
(approximate dating 700 B.C.)
to wake only half a century later.

Who could have told if this bemused old Greek
proved a Van Winkle wiser for his freak
hiatus? Torpor alone, as unsupported feat,
no laddish hero would applaud... Better, perhaps,

to seek newer, less taxing sport, keep free
and fit. The white-haired satyr's an anomaly
allowed an odd boast or a memory lapse,
regretting mislaid dreams and lacking data.

Survival of the Fascist

1
What did you do in World War Two, Daddy?
Were some or any of your best friends Jews?

Were you whatever you claimed, Daddy,
Resistance hero or unwilling baddy?

Were you a bigger wheel, a man misread,
or survivalist, dealer, smalltime crook?

*– Was there what's called 'a good war', or had he
a simple system of lies he'd use?*

It will become far harder to find out,
sift through a crowd of ghosts, the nameless dead.

Hardest to take that tricky backward look,
to write down something – a whisper, a shout.

The echoes linger, thin misleading clues…
When the train's left and the trail's gone cold,

the Jews have all vanished, the fascists too.
Nations are altered now, wage smaller wars instead.

*– Bullying father, might he have been bold,
or was he merely craven, bought and sold?*

But there's much to write and less time to do
justice to myself or you:
grown up at last, grown tired and old,
I've waited long enough to see you out.

2
That German soldier by my cot,
officers billeted in our house,
weren't they a strangely friendly lot?
Naughty man played with a proper gun.
How we laughed to see such fun!

A wireless lay hidden under me –
unlikely story, one more I was told –
so you could tune in to the BBC.
Held by the Gestapo then released?
I discount those fairy tales I was fed.

Everywhere famine made do as a feast.
My mother cycled miles to fetch an egg for me.
The poorer Greeks lay frozen in the streets.
Each morning trucks collected up the dead.
Dad, I don't believe a word you said.

3
So what did you do in the War, Daddy?
Would you do it again, if you could choose?

Back from your deathbed and tell me, Daddy:
I'm closer yet further, there's nothing to lose.

The questions unanswered, avoided, Daddy,
I dare to put here: these you can't now refuse.

The truth that you feared, would you know it again?
Just save the excuses along with your skin,

pious hypocrisy's not the worst sin,
while ashes well scattered can cause no more pain.

– *Your legacy is unasked questions, laddie.*
Neither rhyme nor reason: we do what we're told...

4
Let's not ignore or forget what was done in the War, Daddy.
Hater of inspiration, tone-deaf to any true refrain,
dead and dumb forever you surely must remain.
Yet the bad old days deserve new nursery rhymes.
Even a fortunate child can't readily cope
with the deceptive truth about those bygone times.
It's taken me too long but, reaching sixty-one,

I call you back, mistakenly perhaps... Come now, don't run,
don't fade: speak if you will, old ogre! (Funny how
I'm still here, vainly asking you to take a bow.)
A patriarchal life-span rates applause and, Dad,
a century as near as damn it's what you had.
Survival built on lies. Through their enduring pain
you tried hard not to hang yourself, though given rope.

Voices From the Past

The Allies would soon be done for, thrown out
into the sea. Or so Lord Haw Haw sneered.
Crete had become 'the island of doomed men':
how few are left to recollect that phrase!
Scratch at messages preserved in history's scrapyard,
amid reservoirs of ruined metal, broken wireless sets.
Skull headphones crackling lies, vile static.
The cicada's testament. Distant hiss of hate,
indistinct whispers worse than any shout.

Confrontation with ghosts one has never even met,
let alone dwelt on (and somewhat late in the day)'s
disconcerting. As parlous as absurd,
yet closer to shock than pain. *Be not afeard:
the isle is full of noises...* Each sense may play a trick,
hence one must pay heed, listen, otherwise
no rest is found; regret's a lonely fate.
Keep travelling therefore through this dream-filled sleep,
halfway into vacation, temporary peace.

Perivoli

'Perivoli' (The Garden) is an 18th century mansion set in a paradisiac orange orchard in the heart of Campos on Chios island
Travel brochure

The Campos of Chios is one of the most beautiful and spectacular parts of Greece
G Theotokas

1
From the beginning it occurred to her that revelation
is never what any of us expects, and so a word
of reminder wouldn't go amiss, not
to one in my heightened, anxious state –
unease, excitement mingled. Warned then by her
I loved most that some photographs can turn out
blurred, I feared my hand mightn't remain
steady. The thought and sight of all the beauty
from which I'd been excluded, everything
continuing concealed, never a mention!
Not told before of this sold-off estate,
we couldn't have found it, peered through, or walked
between the great wrought-iron gates
with their scrolled date 1742... There are

recurrent teasing dreams where you find
the Forest of Arden, locate the lost domain
of Alain-Fournier. We imagine, each
of us, a secret garden – or reinvent
secluded Eden, once so briefly glimpsed. To site
it at *6.5 kilometres south of the town of Chios,*
and 3.5 kilometres from the airport and the beach,
seems ecstasy, frustration, anti-climax, simultaneously,
the fable's beginning and end, *a two-storey*
building with wide staircases built with local stones...
No longer the family house, but fairy tale
adapted to the needs of any old traveller,
made to accommodate the tourists we
ourselves in the emptiness of time all turn.

2
Alongside this spacious house ascends
a broad stone staircase. A circular plaque set
into the wall bears a crest, its motto illegible now.
Near another entrance the enormous water-wheel,
the tallest wrought-iron gates. There beneath
the trellis and the blaze of sun at ten, we're served

breakfast in the courtyard. The new owners bought
the place from my family in the Seventies
sometime. Seeming glad to greet us, they give VIP
welcome to this most curious, unsettling sort
of hesitant Hellene – prodigal returned,
who speaks no Greek to speak of, but sails in

from an incomprehensible, far different life,
nervous and smiling with his very English wife...

3
Unwitting and previously uninformed, I reach the place
whose marvellous peace cannot be guessed, a calm kept
hidden, idyllic scene whose pure existence
stayed till the astounding present undisclosed. These
are areas of enchantment, ancient paths criss-crossed
by faded signs marking out secret routes: it could take
a lifetime, too many wasted days to track them down.

Regaining a version of paradise lost
unseen in childhood requires vision of a kind if not
a sacred wood safe for the innocent wanderer. Here's
the door of the story, door in the wall, wide open once
only: a private past, all grounds of an estate that's vanished.
Scent from the citrus groves, a view of vines, rising toward far
hills. Beyond enlightenment it lay and always lies –

thalassa, that truly implausible blue

4
Cradle of aristocratic Chiots. A gracious place and grand,
if not quite Great House, fabled mansion in the sense
that the likes of Yeats and upper crust friends
might have approved. Yet here one vile old villain,
grew up privileged and shown respect
unearned... On this most fertile, lovely island
history and nature seldom left in peace, he lived –
my father – here before the First World War...
Chios hadn't been returned to Greece but then
at the turn of the twentieth century
was a pleasant zone, tranquil heart-land of green
groves. Toward its south-east corner the unique
mastic is still made; acres of lentisk await
their shawled women, black birds picking the trees clean.

My ancestral island lays best claim to being
Homer's birthplace. As chroniclers always said
and Greeks recall, honouring the famous dead
of recent or more distant times... Its landmarks
are memorials of massacre and earthquake, as if they
interpreted certainty, these ruins, the sad
scattered stones whispering of bones concealed,
of lives torn by catastrophe, unnatural greed –
each field and village, every vineyard soaked in blood,
orchards erased. Kindly dust smothers those used
to upheaval: deracinated first, enslaved or slain,
martyrs to the heathen, mere playthings of the Turks...
How long ago, unreal, my adolescence, when I read
but scarcely understood *You Can't Go Home Again!*

5
Across the strait, the port of Smyrna lay, and there
his younger brother my kind Uncle John once swam,
fearlessly buoyant... It was I felt unfortunate
the rollicking and friendly fellow wasn't fated
to be my parent, mentor, truest myth. I'd rather
he'd been the one to call me son and not that
Other, my own sullenly mendacious father.

A differently imagined family tree – what next? I find
myself surrendering to wild surmise and wondering whether
I mightn't have remained in Greece... All ancient history...
The jovial long-dead John lived life more honestly
(dear Yanni, now recalled), as a mere mortal who'd not lie.
He betrayed none, let no one down. And will swim on
here in his element: free spirits never drown.

At Chora Sphakion

One's literary life must turn frequently for sustenance to memories and seek discourse with the shades...
    Joseph Conrad, from 'A familiar Preface' to A Personal Record, 1912

We were never here before. This first time
feels very curiously like coming back.
Whatever fall in place are only shards
of sad research, of recollection shared.
Pictures appear to work by stealth, as I'm
poised over unposted vacation cards,
but memory itself seems to change tack,
leaving me open, mind blank, unprepared,
for harsher flash of vision – sunlit tide,
burst shutters in the *kaffenion* noon.

I've lost sight of the lover at my side.
Partially blinded by laser beam light
that catches knife and traps a tarnished spoon,
I pick up one tantalising sound bite.
Spilt words impossible to get to know
about the fighting and obscure events
of over half a century ago
drift treacherously on... Motes, quotes, fragments,
swirl toward meaning and fade all too soon.
Our histories are also drowned in shadow.

One Side of 'The Family'

    Casdagli reverence for cash need have no earthly bounds:
Thou shalt devoutly cheat close kin on slimy, cozening grounds.
Thieves may believe that money talks and sanctifies all power,
    but I rate disinheritance as much my finest hour.

Old Warrior

My mother's hero and her dearest brother.
Also by far my favourite uncle. Good
godfather of mine, mentor I missed and would
have listened to... Now dwindled to a dim
flame, an ancient namesake – here and not here,
Alexis wrapped in an abstract present. Loss
of memory means stumbling withdrawal into further
frailty, nonagenarian twilight-absence, baffled loneliness.

It's a near-disappearance: at least this cross
borne weighs no heavier than many another.
He's seen to merit a generous, kindly death,
a pain-free passage where, looked after well,
he's done with war. What floats above this sunken shell
need make no waves nor sense. He rests unaware
how much he's loved. His berth already booked. But we
who must remain, go on remembering for him,

loving however clumsily to the last breath.
Meanwhile some spirit flickers – gallantry,
a spark of humour – to encourage our belief
that more is recognised than he lets on.
Retreat is not defeat; the clearer voices he may hear
originate from those far longer gone.
Soon, aboard that final ship, he shall put out to sea,
his weary smile what best endures, combating grief.

First Hand Accounts

Safe after his harrowing experiences
on what became the ritual flight to Egypt
was one beleaguered medic, Theo Stephanides.
This scientist and polymath left a fine account

of the island's tragic Fall: how many
made shift to survive or escaped narrowly,
blundered en route toward a doubtful rescue!
The soldiers struggled an excruciating way

past debris beyond bombed-out Souda Bay,
away from that wrecked base, and on past Chania,
graceful Venetian harbour where
lilacs were mockingly in bloom. They trudged

south over the White Mountains, mile
upon mile of rocky track, scree, hairpin bend.
An endless scramble, while most had to hide
mounting panic, shedding their equipment

as they went, wounded, exhausted and scared.
On their trek, the Stukas kept them company,
strafing the stragglers and the swift alike;
quick or half-dead, it made no sense, no odds.

2.

Wryly, Stephanides chronicled the sheer amount
and weight of surreal weaponry – proven *No Bloody Use.*
For instance, an 'aerial mine-thrower', weird thing,
which supposedly could aim and fling
a net of piano-wire fitted with contact-bombs
to a height of several thousand feet,
thus (by entanglement?) destroying enemy planes.
To work this Heath Robinson device, of course –
with full-scale airborne attack in the offing –
there was no way one could afford to lack
an essential component, namely ammunition.

The Luftwaffe pilots might therefore relax,
themselves not whimsical, nor about to meet
even much flak... So a farewell to false alarms,
rumours of ramshackle great inventions:
these gave way to weight of numbers,
to the brutally real, better-organised force.

Did Stephanides and my uncle meet, I wonder,
somewhere along their shared *via dolorosa*
as far as far-off Chora Sphakion?
Tormented units, shattered remnants, under
those loud guns swooping downward closer
to head them off. Airborne – but thicker on
the ground now – at their heels – too close behind –
hastened the restless pursuer who'd blind
their poor hopes or would cut them short.
That rock or this? Mere flies to German boys
wanting to kill them for their sport,
they sprawled, hid, crouched, ran, staggered from the noise,
yet stumbled somehow, on split-booted bleeding feet,
to the far haven, Chora Sphakion, tiny port
where rescuing Allied ships were due to meet
them. This way or that, too many missed the boat.

3.

So many never made it, so the Doctor wrote.
And as for that good man for whom I'm named,
Alexis – generous unheroic uncle, he
did the brave thing, surrendering his place
in the sun, his safe berth, for a wounded friend...
Years in a German prison camp, until the end
of the war, proved hard reward. When Leck got
home, he purported to be just the same,
though everyone had changed and all put on a show.
Perhaps a certain stubborn pride followed defeat.
(After that hell, a Stalag was a piece of cake.)
He blamed none. Couldn't be discussing Crete.

Such secret histories were *verboten*, so
he'd hint. No kind of story to explain or share...
Those clear, sure things the memory buries deep.
At present they appear to linger on
in his saintly nonagenarian half-sleep
awful and pure, quite as they always were.
Summoned to the surface, never entirely gone,
are gathering forms of utterance that forsake
time altogether, signs of health. Called up again,
they rise, remind him spirit must not break.
Are they epiphanies, the echoes that remain,
a mystery we guess at now, and cannot know?

Afternoon in Anopolis

A taverna in a mountain village,
October afternoon, and nothing much
is moving anywhere. A young girl brings
us salad, beer, rough country bread. We're glad

of it. Time for a break now... The old man
who has materialised from the main square
almost inexorably greets us. We
observe etiquette, answer him slowly,

await stock questions, tell him who we are.
He hears with satisfaction that we're not
German, and only then sits down with us.
Cretan patriarch from some picture book,

clad in tall boots and classic black headgear,
he sets down worn binoculars and shepherd's crook;
pours his crouching, thirsty dog a plate of beer.
We've soon evolved a fractured lingo, things

mainly gestured or guessed, for warmth is what
concerns us here, in heart as on street. An
understanding of how strangers meet, touch,
share the vital shade, and eat and drink

together... We peer at tattered frontage –
metal canopy a grater pattern now where
partying guests had peppered it with shot –
and no one minds, or mends. These folks aren't bad,

(here's what he's struggling to let us know)
they're reckless rather. Long-of-memory...
My mainland family-feuds come back to me;
today's inviolate, though. We rise to leave,

arousing his amused stupefaction:
why should foreigners, Greeks or anyone,
walk so far, even in the waning sun,
when, moreover, there exists a late bus?

Without clear answers we must smile and part –
reckless also, let the old shepherd believe.
And Anopolis recedes as we start
the dizzy zigzag route, with Chora Sphakion
a shimmering vision by an azure sea,
merely kilometres – a dozen – down below.

Goatsong

By dangerous turret
that still threatens collapse
yet crowns

the boulder-strewn outcrop
three herd stragglers have found
tranquil

space to browse off herbs dry
as hillside whose rocks sprout
from ground

so cracked that everything
sunstruck seems to crumble
until

earth in its leisured slide
beneath each scrambling hoof
lets fly

torrents of flat grey stone
cliff-tablets fit to spill
down to

a seething trough of salt
a throne of granite slabs
where sound

flings shingle rhythm to
and fro but will not drown
those bells

tinkling preoccupied
innocent of time and tide
above…

By Souda Bay

Unfinished business, blocks of concrete
offering, bunched at corners,
their inevitable iron
bouquets. It seems these

rusty sprigs are ruins-in-progress,
eyesores passers-by may read
now as 'Notice of Intent',
with every spiky missive

meant to send a certain
signal for the future.
Villas, eventually, await
rubble-free floor or ultimate flat roof,

homes not yet prepared to rise
to their projected heights… Tomorrow,
avrio. Some hope. Nearby apartments though,
sprout also solar panels. Here again

grows bougainvillaea. And whenever peace
is next disturbed, via voices raising Cain,
haughty Teutonic parodies,
loud tenors that *demand* but do not seek

direction/sustenance/relief –
then so be it. Everything is subject
to change, the hollow conquerors too,
raw *Herrenvolk* oblivious of how

their own crude forebears could once wreck
harbour, house or life itself – atrocities
visited upon a poor, proud land.
Invariably, invaders pass: more thoughtful folk give

Crete due credit, lend help, make amends
with holidays well-spent. The hard-pressed islander
will build at all events, live and let live,
extend to wanderers an ancient welcome.

I'm back in love with the forbearing Greeks,
stoics who seldom curse their lot. My long-lost
countrymen whose kind simplicity can move
even a tourist and the far too reticent
and greying stranger I've become.

The Point at Loutro

Over the headland
passing the ruined
turret, goats
pick their ways

between, up round
each dusty rock.
It's just a rock
itself, a rotted

husk. A tube or shell,
some herdsman's
shelter once.
Bare lookout post.

A rough stone
cylinder the years
deprived of roof.
So very far from

the sublime or grand.
An un-Romantic
tower, of course.
But while the herd

takes its own time
to reconnoitre
interesting insects,
aromatic grass,

it's not hard to imagine
Pan lurks in the offing –
euphoric enough,
most happy fellow

with age-old phallus
hard as stone! And thus
The Goatgod's Folly
or perhaps *The Rod*

of Dionysos would
best have suited that odd,
wholly sensual place
with its steep path... Because

we settled for our route
the closest by, and clambered down
the cliff. And shed our clothes
and swam, then chose to rut

right there, rockily blissful, summer goats.
There too we two seemed to hear
(easily recalled, if difficult to tell)
echoes perfectly sweet, saltily clear,
fleeting themes of unearthed treasure,
inklings of every pleasure's carnal bell:

free-floating – scattered wild – confetti spray –
fell scalding noon's moist-petalled tinkling notes.
All round about us and above the bay
music like incense simmered through the day, may still
resound. In pagan places, lost or out of bounds,
it surely beats down, brightly tintinnabulates.

Omonia in the 1960s

Oldtime accounts remark this side of Athens
as given ritually to demonstrations.
But what manifests in memory here's
plain popular survival. Bustling spirit,

just demotic enterprise. Market-stall, patch
and kiosk; pedlar and shoeblack all packed close.
Best rustproof style: your wrought-iron bed-frame, yes?
These fake steel shears? A snip. As used by Atropos.

Wild roaring trade from rickety three-wheelers!
Utter chaos, while the cheap transistors blare...
Pittas, sausage, spit-roast chicken, cheese-
and-spinach pasties. Solid, uncompromising fare

whose spicy heat and scent seem to conspire,
cohere, and hit on every single passer-by,
excess enough to get each tourist high.
Bargain, argument, exchange and curse.

Ikons, oranges or sandals. Local soap,
pistachios, nougat and loukoum.
Leather. And lotteries, the poor last hope.
Sheer noise must surely make some room

in life for them – belief the beggars share.
Meanwhile the fountain goes on playing cooler tricks.
A tramcar struggles past, strikes sparks into
intolerably hot mid-morning air.

2
Along one unappetising alleyway
a frayed strongman, stalwart in grey longjohns,
bends thinnish bits of ironware.
Rousseau, the not-so-naif Douanier,

would have relished his declaratory stance –
absurd red fez and cheeks, brisk gestures, waxed moustache.
Next come some slicker macho men, who by
the custom of the country, arm-in-arm, must mooch

down ever dustier, less savoury side-streets.
Self-conscious strollers with their studied casual glance,
they head for seedy façades, any sad hotel.
A shadow area full of narrow brothels where

harsh-faced broads from old B-movies gossip
on stoops as rough as hash-and-Papastratos...
Smoke-wreathed entrances, smeared grins. Mauve lipstick.
Teeth clicking gold to cap such clapped-out charms.

Bright wraps gape wide and, scornful-slovenly, expose
glimpses of underwear, lace stained and torn.
Or bare limbs, unrestrained: the rare, unsubtle shows
put on only by younger, plumper whores.

Was that the life then – any life at all?
Correctness non-existent, and justice short-changed
through fleeting, fleecing days of neither good
nor ill. Things might have been, could still be, worse...

A time artfully free, before dictatorship.
A place to strip of contrarieties and choice.
Bullyboys flexed new muscle, would come cleaning:
moral folk keen to sell a 'Greece of Christian Greeks'.

ACADEMIC QUESTIONS

> *i.m. C. A. Trypanis (1909-1993)*

1
An avuncular scholarly man
Greek born, whose family came
like mine from Chios. We only met

once in Oxford, late Sixties:
he'd turned absent-minded don.
I can recall a dazzling afternoon

of sunshine, low-key conversation
on elegiac poetry, and coffee.
He seemed awesomely polite,

reticent almost, as I was then
encountering *bona fide* poet.
I'd also heard W. H. Auden,

no less, had greatly praised
his work... At any rate
it prompted a youthful poem,

that day, though I dared not ask
the right questions. Nor would he
have answered them I guess.

Now I regret missed opportunities.
Constantine T. is gone, and look,
I've only myself to blame

for not following up clues
then and there about the War,
for too much reticence about the fates

of friends and relatives, characters I
knew very little of or rarely saw.
Yet paths of wanderers don't cross

when expected, at least not often
enough, so it's been my loss:
the lacunae are all that remain.

2
In a thirty-year-old Eng. Lit. textbook
I spot the familiar Greek name
and what G. S. Fraser (Hellenophile,

another erstwhile poet-academic)
rather encouragingly wrote
of him: "A foreign poet

writing in English may gain
by handling the language with an old-
fashioned simple correctness

and purity." Let's hope he's right,
especially as these fine
sets of initials vanish, the page

alone is left and you go on
trying to move with grace across
it. If some truths get exiled or lost,

others are left still to pursue –
and need finding nonetheless
with a certain style, at whatever cost.

A Diva

i.m. Maria Kalogeropoulou (1923-1977)

Careless or callous? Someone perhaps
with a keen eye to the main chance.
Which sounds more like it. A survivor
at any rate. And now that those concerned
are fewer by the year – most safely dead
or ever less dangerously old –
more controversial stories may be told.
Researches mean that newer, lengthier
biographies are begging to be read.

Fame's heady stuff. As a rising singer,
though US-born, she came to claim whatever
Greek hearts desire, voicing her divine right.
One early rule of life, soon learned,
was to pursue and be pursued
by businessman and potentate –
a form of self-protection, so it seems.
Ambitious self-seeking behaviour
might appear a pardonable lapse

in wartime: sleeping with the enemy,
showbiz rules, dramatic licence and that.
Top C divas obliged at the drop of a hat.
Besides, Maria Callas timed it right,
embracing the allies soon enough.
*'Artists are elitist.' 'Tyros should feel free
to take short cuts in fighting for their dreams.'
'Why blame her if she played tough bitch?'
'Politics become an irrelevance*

*for the chosen few, those born to sing.'
'Adulation shows how she was madly
loved.'* – All questionable arias
that with unrelenting hindsight
don't mean an Ellingtonian thing...
Weight-swings and tantrums apart,
applause and lovers faded, what's quite sadly
apparent? A voice reveals to our ears
often a fatal coarseness, vitiating Art.

The Formalities

> Out of a population of four hundred and fifty thousand, the Cretans, through the fighting and reprisals, lost something like ten thousand men. In spite of all this, one region boasts that, never subdued by previous aggressors, it succeeded in keeping the Germans at bay.
> Edmund Wilson, *Europe Without Baedeker,* 1947

Crete is like Greece in general and so overrun
by foreigners fair or foul, meandering everywhere,
who clog the craft shops that dutifully boast
weavers and silversmiths, an endless quota,

woodworkers, potters, stylists of leatherwear,
bland artists, average artisans, flung together
and indifferently settled on, picked over,
hustlers and hagglers, fleecing or being fleeced

in return, till footsore groups find seats, each one
set to fill restaurant, bar, café where,
proudly displayed, are all these old-style wares
whose newest buyers now avoid the heat

and make comparison of weather
different, extreme, unusually unlike theirs
back in Whateverland, yet their dull stares –
if rarely engaging with the Greeks' – meet

in guilt-free fleeting scorn, the damage done,
wrought on native restlessness ingenuous,
an innocence long-lost without much fuss:
none of us can forego the fun or care

to waste our time counting its mounting cost –
mutual exploitation under unyielding sun.

Albanian Jokes

The corpse of past faith, superseded power,
grows bloated, weightier by the hour
as, grinning chaos fit to burst, it fills
each vacuum created. Envy spills

out into the international weapons store.
One despot gone, if scarcely overthrown,
gives rise to sweeter pipe-dreams – yearning for
land, freedom, even an abandoned throne.

Grim jesters might have drunk to old King Zog
when Stalinist displaced that running dog,
though few there dared pronounce on Enver Hoxha,
endless, efficient villain, evil bodger...

Influx remains the dirty word among Greek friends:
none lightly nor implicitly pretends
a dagger doesn't complement its cloak;
hence nothing's going to happen for the best

in current Balkan politics.
The past has taught the Hellenes colder tricks.
They dread being caught without defence,
and so deploy their well-tried paranoia test.

Ancient scenario: the aliens invade
Greece's mountainous northern border,
or her easier, impossibly inviting seaboard...
(For light years anxious Greeks darkly inveighed

against those shifty neighbours, poorer still
than they were.) Gypsies. Dour Albanian horde,
all half-starved heathen. Barbarous folk
driven more desperate than before...

Ears full of dogma – here's the sickest joke
repeatable – do turn deaf. Nothing's won.
The joy in laughter may be lost. No one
has heard yet of a way to settle or
resolve 'another fine mess', this here fearful fix.

Kneecaps

Likenesses of her, during civil war,
seem lamentably few and far between.
My father ditched whole albums, given away
after her death to favourites he was keen

to impress. Some images endure and form by chance
her unknown grandson's legacy. I hadn't seen
them either: they remind myself today
of all that fall, odd leaps of circumstance.

Here we are, '44. Street battles have begun
when I get that first jolt, the bruise of memory.
My knees bleed. How she's flattened me! Her only son
howls his shocked head off – a raw toddler's misery.

She'd kept her own head, saved us both. So much I saw,
mourning with age, as though I'd never wept before.

Singing Life

> *i.m. Sotiria Bellou, (1922-1997)*

1
Hear her, be haunted
by the way she sings
her fierce lament, this song
of poverty and dispossession
the strange but true Greek blues

Wild hashish music swirling
in from Asia Minor
art of the displaced,
pride restored to immigrants
yearning for lost heartlands

Lyrics of hunger and sex
hunger for sex and love
with despair in its wake
followed by inexorable
black-shawled death

Such wayward threnodies
were always hard-earned
for, according to another
of the pioneer musicians,
their style, *rembetika,* is learned

straight from life 'by someone
who had a sorrow and threw it out'

2
A sullen photo of her stares out
at us from the sun-faded page
of a book read years ago on Crete.
Sotiria Bellou, finest of them all,
lived hard and knew hard times.
And did time, yet without defeat
since that first sentence in her teens:
a young girl wanting to endure no more
assaults from her unfaithful
brutishly drunken husband...

For vitriol flung at the man she got
vilification, six months' jail. Branded
black sheep and whore, disowned by
genteel family – she sang. Some maintain
it was vile left wing sympathies
indecent lesbian leanings which
landed the singer in this and later
worse predicaments. Be that as it may

Sotiria Bellou, who remained a true
street-fighting woman, would recognise
nothing morally in common here
with that band of little English
rock stars, millionaires of today
who in their safer times were lauded
largely for raw swagger, for being a bland
society's licensed minstrels, bad spoilt boys.

In the 1940s Athens I hear,
if scarcely recall, it is she who survives –
Sotiria, compulsive gambler, partisan,
courageous woman wounded by
a British mortar shell, who shrugs off pain
and torture and goes on to sing
immortally of the poor flesh: how great
the spirit called for, to enrich our lives!

3
Some Nazi-loving Greeks attacked
her in 1948 as she refused to sing
for them – then these collaborators
treated her to a further shameful beating

A woman ever generous to
other musicians, to the poor, to friends,
generous to a fault perhaps
if that phrase proves or means a thing

In 1941 Billie Holiday sang *Gloomy Sunday*
'the Hungarian suicide song' –
Bellou in '48 is listed as recording
an equally grim lyric *Cloudy Sunday*

Kindred spirits, a resilient trio –
Bessie, Billie, Bellou –
singers of great presence
battlers against odds, alert

to lies of language. Bellou
is a key survivor here: her
difficult life far longer than
her sisterly predecessors'

though in her case the final years
were harshly silenced by
throat cancer. Bullied out of every lyric,
she'd have felt cheated, dealt that card of doom

which saw off yet another distinctive
gambler misfit – Cavafis the sardonic,
my distant kin… Gone those poetic voices,
all unknown allies, undefeated talents:

they couldn't work a way round fate's worst trick.
Perhaps such personal odysseys may give
anyone able to accept it something
rare, an unfamiliar music to rejoice

to, that resounds within the heart: the dream
most artful, careless love both rough and smooth.
So once upon a bruising, vanished time
soul took on flesh and found a lonely voice.

Civil Wars Are Worst

> Blood brings blood and more blood
> *George Seferis, Diary 1945-51*

Memoirs from faded diaries, stubbornly breathing courage,
induce, by belated translation, pride in being born Greek.
Just as shame and indignant pity soon displace outrage
on reading of barbarity one's countrymen could wreak.

Thousands deported to Makronisos, Ai-Strati and Trikeri,
those island prison camps of which new democrats no longer speak,
where all women were equal, tortured together or dying solitary,
beaten, raped, wracked with hunger and TB. They were not weak

and few of this weaker sex signed any Declaration
of Repentance: partisans, ex-Resistants, students, Communists,
peasants, families of *andartes*. Hellish years. No recantation
meant the routine of suffering continued. Those clenched fists

raised high their own spirits if not the allied dead betrayed.
Churchill, Stalin, fair weather friends, had left them in the lurch.
So what did women fight tyranny for? After all they'd paid
with their blood to win a dream… Democracy – that broad church

too often pardoning collabos, fascists, hypocrites –
holds blithely to the hope that old wounds will heal as the past
is obscured. Memory persists: a grinning jailer shits
on the grave of a former scapegoat. How long must it last,

righteous accommodating hate? Slaves of the status quo,
who hear a present whisper of such things, won't care to weep,
but might interrogate themselves to pay off debts they owe
their ancestors. The night is shared with ghosts that never sleep.

INTERROGATION

When did you last see your father?
Early 1970.
How old can that old hypocrite be?
96 now, and still fit.
*Why are all villains long-lived, and isn't it
telling, this Greek tragedy twist?* A rather
protracted estrangement, true,
but sheer self-preservation dictates a course to you
and you take off, though further debts must next be paid
before those most unwelcome memories fade.

I summon up the man beset by guilt
   and yet devoid of shame, the one
unwilling to attend my mother's funeral.
   The man who told me, too late, she was dying,
so when I flew from France to find her in a coma
   my grief became too great to admit anger:
I stood alone, left to shake hands with strangers.

At 23, my own determinedly earnest mask
   of struggling writer, dutiful only son,
hid that new boy aged 6, at school up north,
   needing to learn an unfamiliar language fast.
One more mockable alien whose main task
   upon arrival was simply to fit in, not
be singled out as strange, and to forget the past
   however short. Yet nonchalance fools none.

Again, he wasn't *there* – therefore my smaller self
   showed fatherless, fair game, and bore already marks
of difference: the foreign name; thin brittle bones
   of the malnourished; rickets; thyroid and glandular
imbalances; the respiration problems. But I'd got
   clear of Occupation, Civil War: how fortunate
to be alive! I owed my mother this new life, since she
   had sensibly divorced him, hurried home at last
to relatives in England, clinging obstinate
   to British passport and her troubled child.

And what became of him, back in that land you were
now desperately trying to forget?

He never had to pay too high a price,
    could justify black market moves, collaboration,
whatever else he did and wouldn't later mention,
    as buying freedom for his family...
For me, he turned into The Enemy,
    returned to England to remarry her –
a crafty postwar ruse to flee disgrace,
    acquire authority and nationality;
next, having won her round, required of me
    my silence, love, respect, obedience
and all instinctively I could not give.

I feared, distrusted him throughout
    this new or 'second' childhood while the Greek
beginnings were being left behind.
    Quite soon I faced a total absence
of recall, a memory-block that even now
    I'm most loath to confront, still less disturb...
He remained, I remember, In-The-Right.
    The man who physically resembled Mussolini,
the fascist seeming pledged to blight my youth,
    the man my mother must appease, restrain,
when in a beating mood with belt unlooped.
    Finicky patriarch, who'd confiscate my toys
and shout at me for making too much noise,
    he never deigned to tell the bitter truth.

His cold and negative example taught me well.
    I've tried to do the very opposite in life,
believing in real loyalty and love – it's hell
    on earth only *pretending* to. And I found strife
can steel the soul, for if you lose one fight
    there's always next time: you might win the war.
Whatever's stolen from you you must not regret –
    each true guerrilla travels swift and light before
the burdened tyrant meets that last sunset.

Plausible too, a dabbler in the occult.
    Among the earliest Scientologists,
a would-be guru who despised the world.
    Marching to his own different, selfish drum,
he always needed others to control...
    Motherless, I was easier to manipulate,
even moved to pity for him: his feigned grief
    at her death shouldn't have fooled me, but hate
seemed inappropriate then. It was beyond belief
    how he had once hired a psychiatrist
to rule in favour of rude shocks for me –
    that fashionable barbarity of ECT.

But such a dubious course, both claimed, was best!
    No choice nor consultation did they offer me:
I was a minor then, and rescued by
    my mother's staunch resistance. (She would pay
for such good sense until her dying day.)
    A tame teenage revolt was all one knew
in those grey 1950s... My supposed
    lunacy must have suited, soothed him, too:
there lurked a fear or a fierce jealousy
    within him of what I'd grow up to do.

Their correspondence I once chanced to read
    years later – though naively never kept
the damning proof. Instead, I tried to see
    some good in him, agreed to share a flat
with the unctuous widower, till even that
    act of mistaken filial piety
turned sour, became impossibility.
    He labelled me a junkie, and yet leapt
to more correct conclusions – scenting demon weed,
    my girlfriend's Guerlain – freedoms dangerous indeed.
She was that beauty whom unwittingly
    in a smart restaurant he chatted up,
saw fit to ogle over coffee cup...

Sublime coincidence of comedy!
Identities mistaken to the end... We see
    the point at which one routs the enemy.
No more jail, an end to that control-freak
    whose two or three crazily vicious letters
over the years are his sole legacy to me.
    Lover of money, selfishness incarnate, he
will never get to read my final word
    here. Betrayal means a life in fetters.
Treasure your birthright as a Greek. Stay free.

Last Respects

1

Ten years ago I reached the age at which you died.
It never seemed a fulfilled lifetime span.
I grew up unaware my father lied,
or that you'd twice been bride and dupe of such a man.

I recollect how short a life you had,
and hindsight sends me back those hours I spent
with you, however few they were, when nothing bad
could cloud our spirits. At such times I meant

to speak of love, but did not. Brutal circumstance,
ill-health and a resentful husband, silenced you.
On borrowed money, in a panic, I flew back from France
to find you comatose, the shell of you...

2

A final coldness, his feigned sorrow. He believed
now she'd remain a fool for good and all, stay dumb.
Distant acquaintances took pains to show up, grieved,
sharing a sadness far beyond the crematorium.

To that last place he didn't care to come –
merely a mile by car – so I alone
shook strangers' hands and talked of Mum
and made excuses for his heart of stone.

If it were proved a god existed I might pray
that there should be a showdown and a way
of telling some home truths on Judgement Day.